Anonymous

Centennial Album of Nashville, Tennessee

Containing exposition buildings officers of the exposition, representative citizens, public buildings, business houses, and private residences

Anonymous

Centennial Album of Nashville, Tennessee
Containing exposition buildings officers of the exposition, representative citizens, public buildings, business houses, and private residences

ISBN/EAN: 9783337152048

Printed in Europe, USA, Canada, Australia, Japan

Cover: Foto ©ninafisch / pixelio.de

More available books at **www.hansebooks.com**

CENTENNIAL ALBUM

OF

NASHVILLE. TENNESSEE

CONTAINING

EXPOSITION BUILDINGS.

OFFICERS OF THE EXPOSITION.

REPRESENTATIVE CITIZENS.

PUBLIC BUILDINGS.

BUSINESS HOUSES.

AND

PRIVATE RESIDENCES.

PREPARED BY

J. PROUSNITZER & COMPANY.

1896.

... Introductory

THE first intention of the publisher of the Centennial Album was to present to the public the pictures of the buildings and officers of the forthcoming Tennessee Centennial Exposition. As the work progressed, however, it was decided to add to these the pictures of some of Nashville's prominent citizens, as well as its public buildings, business houses, churches, and private residences.

While this work contains only a small part of what might be given, it nevertheless enables the stranger to form some idea of the importance of the city of Nashville.

J. PROUSNITZER,
PUBLISHER.

J. W. THOMAS,

PRESIDENT NASHVILLE, CHATTANOOGA & ST. LOUIS RAILWAY COMPANY
AND
PRESIDENT TENNESSEE CENTENNIAL EXPOSITION.

ADMINISTRATION BUILDING.

FREDERICK THOMPSON, DEL.

VAN L. KIRKMAN.

FIRST VICE PRESIDENT TENNESSEE CENTENNIAL EXPOSITION.

PHOTO BY OTTO GIERS. DUDLEY, ARCHITECT.

JACKSON BUILDING.

GEN. W. H. JACKSON.

PHOTO BY OTTO GIERS.

COLE BUILDING.

PHOTO BY CALVERT BROS. & TAYLOR.

E. W. COLE.

TRANSPORTATION BUILDING.

PHOTO BY OTTO GIERS.

A. W. WILLS,
COMMISSIONER GENERAL TENNESSEE CENTENNIAL EXPOSITION.

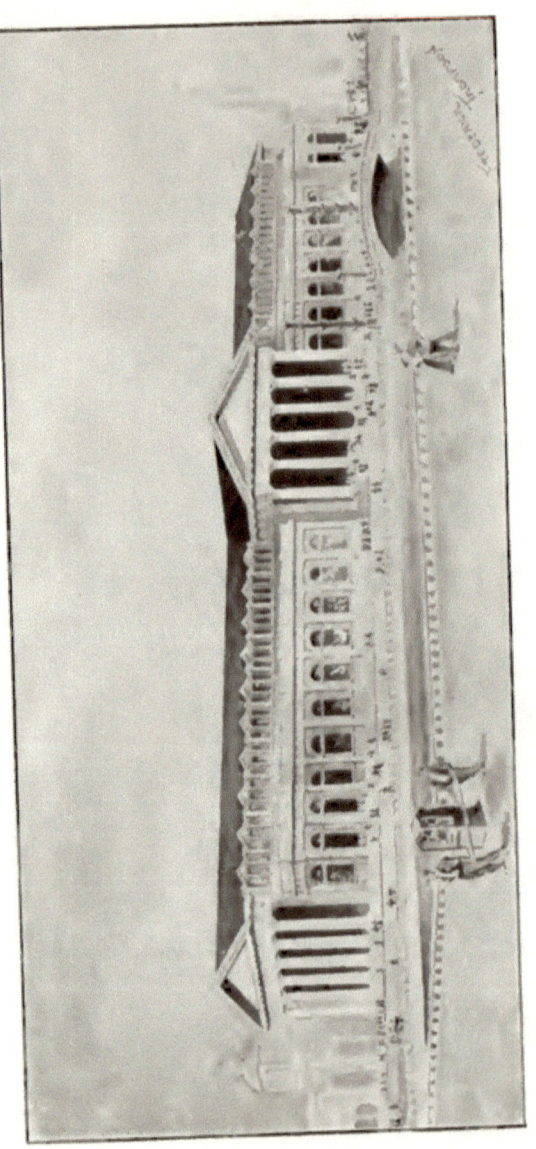

MACHINERY BUILDING.

FREDERICK THOMPSON. DEL.

PHOTO BY OTTO GIERS.

W. F. FOSTER.

AGRICULTURAL BUILDING.

JUL. G. ZWICKER, ARCHITECT.

AUGUSTUS H. ROBINSON.
VICE PRESIDENT UNION BANK AND TRUST COMPANY.

FREDERICK THOMPSON, DEL.

AUDITORIUM.

B. F. WILSON.

FINE ARTS BUILDING. (THE PARTHENON.)

FREDERICK THOMPSON. DEL.

PHOTO BY OTTO GIERS.

THEODORE COOLEY.

CHIEF DEPARTMENT OF FINE ARTS.

SARA WARD-CONLEY, ARTIST, ARCHITECT.

WOMAN'S BUILDING.

PHOTO BY OTTO GIERS.

SARA WARD-CONLEY.

ARTIST.

CHILDREN'S BUILDING.

PHOTO BY OTTO GIERS.

W. T. DAVIS.
CHIEF CHILDREN'S DEPARTMENT, TENNESSEE CENTENNIAL.

COMMERCE BUILDING.
FREDERICK THOMPSON, DEL.

PHOTO BY OTTO GIERS.

J. B. KILLEBREW, A. M., PH. D.,

COMMISSIONER OF AGRICULTURE FOR THE STATE OF TENNESSEE FROM 1871 TO 1881, AND SPECIAL EXPERT OF THE TENTH CENSUS, AND ONE OF THE WRITERS OF THE STANDARD DICTIONARY.

PHOTO BY CALVERT BROS. & TAYLOR.
THOS. D. FITE.

PHOTO BY OTTO GIERS.

JOHN D. ANDERSON.

PHOTO BY CALVERT BROS. & TAYLOR.

T. F. P. ALLISON.
COMMISSIONER OF AGRICULTURE, STATE OF TENNESSEE.

PHOTO BY OTTO GIERS.

G. P. THRUSTON,
PRESIDENT STATE INSURANCE COMPANY.

PHOTO BY OTTO GIERS.

F. T. CUMMINS,
PRESIDENT SOUTHERN SODA WORKS.

THOS. A. ATCHISON, M. D.

RESIDENCE OF JOHN A. WARD.

PHOTO BY OTTO GIERS.

PHOTO BY OTTO GIERS.

JOHN A. WARD.

GENERAL AGENT KENTUCKY WAGON MANUFACTURING COMPANY.
DIRECTOR TENNESSEE CENTENNIAL.

TENNESSEE INDUSTRIAL SCHOOL.

PHOTO BY CALVERT BROS. & TAYLOR.

PHOTO BY CALVERT BROS. & TAYLOR.

W. C. KILVINGTON.
SUPERINTENDENT TENNESSEE INDUSTRIAL SCHOOL.

RESIDENCE OF MAYOR WM. M. McCARTHY.

PHOTO BY OTTO GIERS.

PHOTO BY OTTO GIERS.

WM. M. McCARTHY.
MAYOR OF THE CITY OF NASHVILLE.

PHOTO BY OTTO GIERS.

FACTORY OF THE HILL TRUNK COMPANY.

J. L. HILL.
MANAGER HILL TRUNK COMPANY

SALESROOM B. H. STIEF JEWELRY COMPANY.

PHOTO BY OTTO GIERS.

PHOTO BY OTTO GIERS.

JAMES B. CARR,
MANAGER B. H. STIEF JEWELRY COMPANY.

INTERIOR OF MAX BLOOMSTEIN'S PHARMACY.

PHOTO BY OTTO GIERS.

PHOTO BY OTTO GIERS.

MAX BLOOMSTEIN,
PHARMACIST AND CHEMIST.

PHOTO BY OTTO GIERS.

J. K. HEMPHILL,
PRESIDENT POST B. TRAVELERS' PROTECTIVE ASSOCIATION
OF AMERICA.

JAMES GEDDES.
SUPERINTENDENT LOUISVILLE & NASHVILLE RAILROAD.

PHOTO BY OTTO GIERS.

GEO. C. PORTER,
PRESIDENT STATE BOARD OF ASSESSORS AND EQUALIZERS.

DUNCAN EVE. M. D.

PHOTO BY OTTO GIERS.

JUL. G. ZWICKER,

ARCHITECT.

JNO. C. FERRIS,
COUNTY JUDGE DAVIDSON COUNTY.

PHOTO BY OTTO GIERS.

R. A. YOUNG.
REGENT BELMONT COLLEGE.

PHOTO BY OTTO GIERS.

T. I. WEBB.
OF SPURLOCK-NEAL COMPANY, WHOLESALE DRUGGISTS.

MAXWELL HOUSE, W. K. BLACK, MANAGER.

PHOTO BY OTTO GIERS.

PHOTO BY OTTO GIERS.

U. S. CUSTOM HOUSE.

RESIDENCE OF POSTMASTER H. J. CHENEY.

PHOTO BY OTTO GIERS.

PHOTO BY OTTO GIERS.

H. J. CHENEY.
POSTMASTER, NASHVILLE.

PHOTO BY CALVERT BROS. & TAYLOR.

THOMAS L. MADDIN, M. D.

S. F. WILSON.
JUDGE COURT OF CHANCERY APPEALS.

PHOTO BY OTTO GIERS.

W. B. WALTON, JR.
NASHVILLE'S HATTER. SOLE AGENT DUNLAP'S HATS
AND MILLER'S HATS.

PHOTO BY OTTO GIERS.

BEN LINDAUER,
OF HERMAN BROS., LINDAUER & CO., WHOLESALE DRY GOODS AND BOOTS AND SHOES.

CENTRAL BAPTIST CHURCH.

PHOTO BY OTTO GIERS.

PHOTO BY OTTO GIERS.

REV. GEO. A. LOFTON,
PASTOR CENTRAL BAPTIST CHURCH.

RESIDENCE OF JUDGE JOHN WOODARD AND JOHN H. WOODARD, M. D.

PHOTO BY OTTO GIERS.

JUDGE JOHN WOODARD.

PHOTO BY OTTO GIERS.

A. J. HARRIS,
CIRCUIT COURT CLERK DAVIDSON COUNTY.

PHOTO BY OTTO GIERS.

JOHN H. WOODARD, M. D.

RESIDENCE OF R. L. WEAKLEY.

PHOTO BY CALVERT BROS. & TAYLOR.

PHOTO BY CALVERT BROS. & TAYLOR.

R. L. WEAKLEY.

PHOTO BY OTTO GIERS.

HENRY J. DUDLEY,
ARCHITECT JACKSON BUILDING.

W. L. NICHOL, M. D.

PHOTO BY OTTO GIERS.

JAMES A. YOWELL,
GENERAL AGENT UNION CENTRAL LIFE INSURANCE COMPANY.

PHOTO BY OTTO GIERS.

JAMES TAYLOR.
GENERAL INSURANCE AGENT.

DR. WM. WHITE,
OF WHITE, DUDLEY & CO., BANKERS.

PHOTO BY CALVERT BROS. & TAYLOR.

FRANK B. FOGG.

GENERAL MANAGER DUCK RIVER PHOSPHATE COMPANY.

WAREROOMS JESSE FRENCH PIANO AND ORGAN COMPANY.

PHOTO BY OTTO GIERS.

PHOTO BY OTTO GIERS.

C. A. LITTERER,
OF FIRM OF C. A. LITTERER & CO., DEALERS IN FARM IMPLEMENTS.

WAREROOM OF J. W. CAMP, SEWING MACHINES AND BIRDS.

PHOTO BY OTTO GIERS.

P. A. SHELTON.
COUNTY COURT CLERK DAVIDSON COUNTY.

PHOTO BY OTTO GIERS

J. B. ARMSTRONG,
REGISTER DAVIDSON COUNTY.

PHOTO BY CALVERT BROS. & TAYLOR.

W. A. ATCHISON. M. D.

PHOTO BY CALVERT BROS. & TAYLOR.

D. C. KELLEY,
REV. AND D. D., NEE COL. CAVALRY, C. S. A.

PHOTO BY CALVERT BROS. & TAYLOR.

JNO. W. MORTON.
ASSISTANT COMMISSIONER OF AGRICULTURE.

PHOTO BY OTTO GIERS.

W. D. COVINGTON,
ATTORNEY FOR DAVIDSON COUNTY.

PHOTO BY OTTO GIERS.

J. L. ATKINS.
THE PIONEER HORSE SHOER.

CHRIST CHURCH (EPISCOPAL.)

PHOTO BY OTTO GIERS.

PHOTO BY OTTO GIERS.

REV. JAMES R. WINCHESTER, D. D.
RECTOR OF CHRIST CHURCH.

PHOTO BY OTTO GIERS.

W. T. LINCK,
PROPRIETOR LINCK'S HOTEL.

PHOTO BY OTTO GIERS.

C. H. SANDERS,
GENERAL AGENT LOUISVILLE & NASHVILLE R. R.

PHOTO BY OTTO GIERS.

ALEXANDER FALL.
PRESIDENT NASHVILLE SHORTHAND INSTITUTE.

PHOTO BY OTTO GIERS.

S. G. GILBREATH.
STATE SUPERINTENDENT PUBLIC INSTRUCTION.

TENNESSEE SCHOOL FOR THE BLIND.

PHOTO BY OTTO GIERS.

PHOTO BY OTTO GIERS.

DAVID LIPSCOMB, JR.
SUPERINTENDENT TENNESSEE SCHOOL FOR THE BLIND.

PHOTO BY OTTO GIERS.

CHAS. S. MARTIN,
OF SPURLOCK-NEAL COMPANY, WHOLESALE DRUGS.

PHOTO BY CALVERT BROS. & TAYLOR.

JAMES B. STEPHENS. M. D.

PHOTO BY OTTO GIERS.

JAS. H. JAMISON,
Gen'l State Agent of the Michigan Mutual Life Ins. Co.
Detroit, Michigan.

PHOTO BY OTTO GIERS.

M. M. KLINE,
OF KLINE & CRUZEN REAL ESTATE CO.
AND PRESIDENT GRANDVIEW LAND CO.

PHOTO BY OTTO GIERS.

DEPARTMENT OF DENTISTRY,
VANDERBILT UNIVERSITY.

PHOTO BY CALVERT BROS. & TAYLOR.

W. H. MORGAN, M. D., D. D. S.
DEAN OF THE DEPARTMENT OF DENTISTRY,
VANDERBILT UNIVERSITY.

PHOTO BY OTTO GIERS.

FRANK W. GREEN,
FIRE, LIFE AND ACCIDENT INSURANCE.

PHOTO BY CALVERT BROS. & TAYLOR.

DR. HENRY W. MORGAN.

RESIDENCE OF JUDGE HORACE H. LURTON.

PHOTO BY BRANDON PRINTING CO.

HORACE H. LURTON,
JUDGE UNITED STATES COURT OF APPEALS.

PHOTO BY OTTO GIERS.

WEST END CHURCH.

PHOTO BY OTTO GIERS.

REV. J. B. ERWIN,
PASTOR WEST END M. E. CHURCH SOUTH, 1895.

UNIVERSITY OF NASHVILLE—CHAPEL.

PHOTO BY OTTO GIERS.

PHOTO BY OTTO GIERS.

W. H. PAYNE, LL. D.
CHANCELLOR AND PRESIDENT UNIVERSITY OF NASHVILLE
AND PEABODY NORMAL COLLEGE.

PHOTO BY OTTO GIERS.

CASTLE HALL OF JOEL A. BATTLE LODGE, No. 84,
KNIGHTS OF PYTHIAS.

PHOTO BY OTTO GIERS.

W. R. PAYNE.

SECRETARY AND TREASURER UNIVERSITY OF NASHVILLE
AND PEABODY NORMAL COLLEGE.

PHOTO BY CALVERT BROS. & TAYLOR.

DAVID M. SMITH,
MANAGER PUBLISHING HOUSE OF THE M. E. CHURCH SOUTH.

PHOTO BY CALVERT BROS. & TAYLOR.

DR. J. D. BARBEE,
AGENT PUBLISHING HOUSE OF THE M. E. CHURCH SOUTH.

PHOTO BY OTTO GIERS.

C. S. LILLIE,
CONTRACTOR AND BUILDER.

PHOTO BY OTTO GIENS.

J. CRUM EPLER, M. D.

"MELROSE," RESIDENCE OF G. M. FOGG.

PHOTO BY OTTO GIERS.

PHOTO BY OTTO GIERS.

RESIDENCE OF F. M. HAMILTON.
PRESIDENT INDIANA LUMBER CO.

PHOTO BY OTTO GIERS.

CHAS. FRANKLAND,
WHOLESALE NOTIONS, WHITE GOODS, AND GENTS' FURNISHINGS.

PHOTO BY OTTO GIERS.

CHURCH A. ALLEN.
MANAGER REINECKE COAL COMPANY.

INTERIOR OF L. R. FREEMAN & CO.'S STORE.

WALL PAPER, MIRRORS, AND DECORATIONS.

PHOTO BY OTTO GIERS.

PHOTO BY OTTO GIERS.

L. R. FREEMAN.
THE WALL PAPER PIONEER.

RESIDENCE OF B. J. McCARTHY.

PHOTO BY OTTO GIERS.

PHOTO BY OTTO GIERS.

B. J. McCARTHY,
SUPERINTENDENT PHILLIPS & BUTTORFF MANUFACTURING COMPANY.

PHOTO BY OTTO GIERS.

JOHN M. PICTON.
FIRE AND LIFE UNDERWRITER.

PHOTO BY OTTO GIERS.

GUS DEMERICH.

PLUMBING, GAS AND STEAM FITTING CONTRACTOR.

PHOTO BY OTTO GIERS.

JOHN D. BRIEN.

ATTORNEY AT LAW.

PHOTO BY OTTO GIERS.

CHARLES BREYER,
Pioneer in the Russian and Turkish Bath Business.

PHOTO BY OTTO GIERS.

CUMBERLAND PRESBYTERIAN PUBLISHING HOUSE.

PHOTO BY OTTO GIERS.

JOHN M. GAUT.

ATTORNEY FOR AMERICAN NATIONAL BANK.
AND
GENERAL MANAGER OF PUBLISHING WORK OF CUMBERLAND
PRESBYTERIAN CHURCH.

PHOTO BY BRANDON PRINTING COMPANY.

ELM STREET M. E. CHURCH, SOUTH.

PHOTO BY OTTO GIERS.

REV. W. T. HAGGARD,
PASTOR ELM STREET M. E. CHURCH, SOUTH.

PHOTO BY OTTO GIERS.

THOS. CALLENDER,
SOUTHERN AGENT LAFLIN & RAND POWDER COMPANY.

PHOTO BY OTTO GIERS.

F. S. KINNAIRD,
MANAGER POSTAL TELEGRAPH COMPANY.

PHOTO BY BRANDON PRINTING COMPANY.

THE BANNER BUILDING.

PHOTO BY OTTO GIERS.

EDGAR M. FOSTER.

BUSINESS MANAGER OF THE NASHVILLE BANNER.

GIDEON H. BASKETTE.
EDITOR-IN-CHIEF OF THE NASHVILLE BANNER.

MR. E. B. STAHLMAN.

PHOTO BY BRANDON PRINTING COMPANY.

THE AMERICAN NATIONAL BANK BUILDING.

PHOTO BY BRANDON PRINTING COMPANY.

THE FOURTH NATIONAL BANK BUILDING.

RESIDENCE OF VAN L. KIRKMAN.

PHOTO BY OTTO GIERS.

PHOTO BY OTTO GIERS.

EDWARD LAURENT,
CONTRACTOR AND BUILDER.

ST. CECILIA ACADEMY.

CONDUCTED BY DOMINICAN SISTERS.

PHOTO BY OTTO GIERS.

PHOTO BY OTTO GIERS.

C. LARSEN.

MANUFACTURER OF PICTURE FRAMES.

SALESROOM OF CHAS. THURMAN & CO.

PHOTO BY OTTO GIERS.

PHOTO BY OTTO GIERS.

CHAS. THURMAN,
The Clothier.

PHOTO BY BRANDON PRINTING COMPANY.

NASHVILLE COLLEGE FOR YOUNG LADIES.

REV. GEO. W. F. PRICE, D. D.
PRESIDENT NASHVILLE COLLEGE FOR YOUNG LADIES.

PHOTO BY OTTO GIERS.

THOMAS H. WEBB,
OF DUBOIS & WEBB, AGENTS FOR THE ELECTROPOISE.

JOHN E. DUBOIS.
OF DUBOIS & WEBB, AGENTS FOR THE ELECTROPOISE.

CENTRAL TENNESSEE COLLEGE.

PHOTO BY OTTO GIERS.

J. BRADEN, D. D.
PRESIDENT CENTRAL TENNESSEE COLLEGE.

PHOTO BY OTTO GIERS.

HENRY KLEIN,
BUILDING INSPECTOR, CITY OF NASHVILLE.

PHOTO BY CALVERT BROS. & TAYLOR.

LOUIS G. PALABOT.

PRINCIPAL NASHVILLE SCHOOL OF LANGUAGES.

RETAIL SALESROOM OF THE H. A. FRENCH CO.
PHOTO BY OTTO GIERS.

PHOTO BY OTTO GIERS.

WILLCOX BUILDING.

1894.

BAILEY & TOBIN, MERCHANT TAILORS.

PHOTO BY OTTO GIERS.

REV. E. M. CRAVATH, D. D.
PRESIDENT FISK UNIVERSITY.

BRUTON & CONDON'S SNUFF MANUFACTURING ESTABLISHMENT.

PHOTO BY OTTO GIERS.

JERE BAXTER.

PHOTO BY OTTO GIERS.

RESIDENCE OF W. V. DAVIDSON.

GENERAL MANAGER THE W. V. DAVIDSON LUMBER COMPANY.

PHOTO BY OTTO GIERS.

W. V. DAVIDSON.
GENERAL MANAGER THE W. V. DAVIDSON LUMBER COMPANY.

PHOTO BY OTTO GIERS.

LEWIS F. BUTLER,
GENERAL AGENT MASSACHUSETTS BENEFIT LIFE ASSOCIATION,
BOSTON, MASS.

PHOTO BY OTTO GIERS.

GRACE CUMBERLAND PRESBYTERIAN CHURCH.

PHOTO BY OTTO GIERS.

REV. W. T. RODGERS.
PASTOR GRACE CUMBERLAND PRESBYTERIAN CHURCH.

RESIDENCE OF CHAS. H. SWEENEY.

PHOTO BY OTTO GIERS.

SALESROOM OF HUNTINGTON, CLOTHIER.

H. A. HUNTINGTON.

PHOTO BY OTTO GIERS

PROPERTY OF M. H. CARTWRIGHT.

PHOTO BY OTTO GIERS.

M. H. CARTWRIGHT,
DEALER IN REAL ESTATE.

OFFICE AND WORKS NASHVILLE LAUNDRY CO.

LEO D. WEGE.
PROPRIETOR NASHVILLE LAUNDRY COMPANY.

FREDERIC EMERSON FARRAR.
VOCAL TEACHER AND COMPOSER.

PHOTO BY OTTO GIERS.

J. H. CURREY, M. D.
ASSISTANT POSTMASTER, NASHVILLE, TENN.

RETAIL DEPARTMENT OF J. H. FALL & CO.

SALESROOM OF SPURLOCK-NEAL COMPANY,
WHOLESALE DRUGGISTS.

THE AMERICAN.

PHOTO BY OTTO GIERS.

JONAS TAYLOR,
THE HORSESHOER.

W. G. SADLER.
GENERAL MANAGER NATIONAL FERTILIZER COMPANY.

PHOTO BY CALVERT BROS. & TAYLOR.

WHARTON J. ALLEN.

PHOTO BY CALVERT BROS. & TAYLOR

CHAS. P. ELLIS,
OF FIRM OF J. ELLIS, CLOTHIER AND HATTER.

PHOTO BY OTTO GIERS.

C. S. BRIGGS, M. D.

PHOTO BY CALVERT BROS. & TAYLOR.

MAJ. A. L. LANDIS,
PRESIDENT LANDIS INVESTMENT BANKING COMPANY.

PHOTO BY OTTO GIERS.

J. H. SMITH.
MANAGER MASSACHUSETTS LIFE INSURANCE COMPANY.

RESIDENCE OF HAMILTON PARKS, ESQ.

PHOTO BY OTTO GIERS.

HAMILTON PARKS.
ATTORNEY AT LAW.

THOS. MENEES, M. D.
PROFESSOR OBSTETRICAL DEPARTMENT, VANDERBILT UNIVERSITY.

P. M. ESTES.
ATTORNEY AT LAW.

JO. LINDAUER,
OF HERMAN BROS., LINDAUER & CO., WHOLESALE DRY GOODS AND
BOOTS AND SHOES.

PHOTO BY CALVERT BROS. & TAYLOR.

ALBERT S. WILLIAMS,
PRESIDENT CITY COUNCIL AND CASHIER CITY SAVINGS BANK.

PHOTO BY CALVERT BROS. & TAYLOR.

WALTER M. DAKE, M. D.

PHOTO BY CALVERT BROS. & TAYLOR.

WM. C. DAKE, M. D.

PHOTO BY OTTO GIERS.

G. N. TILLMAN,
ATTORNEY AT LAW.

PHOTO BY OTTO GIERS.

EDWARD H. EAST,
ATTORNEY AT LAW.

PHOTO BY OTTO GIERS

JOHN A. PITTS,
ATTORNEY AT LAW.

PHOTO BY OTTO GIERS.

NAT. BAXTER, JR.
PRESIDENT TENNESSEE COAL, IRON & RAILROAD COMPANY.

PHOTO BY OTTO GIERS.

W. W. CORE, M. D.
DAVIDSON COUNTY HEALTH OFFICER.

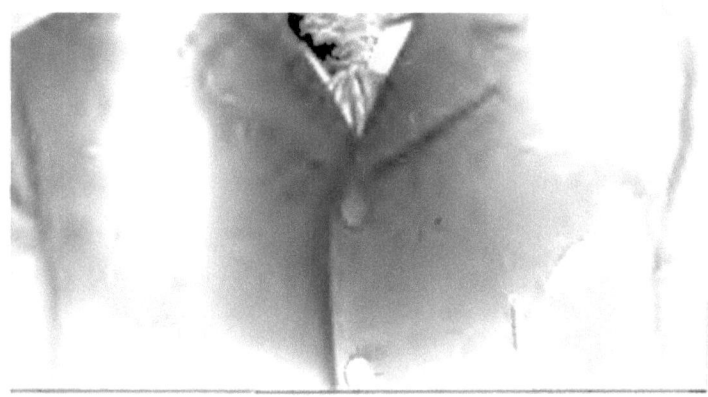

PHOTO BY CALVERT BROS. & TAYLOR.

ANDREW JACKSON CASEY.

GENERAL MANAGER FOR WEST AND MIDDLE TENNESSEE FOR THE NATIONAL LIFE ASSOCIATION OF HARTFORD, CONN.

INTERIOR OF GIERS' ART GALLERY.

HENRY GIBEL,
ARCHITECT MACHINERY BUILDING.

PHOTO BY BRANDON PRINTING COMPANY.

BRANDON PRINTING COMPANY,
ENGRAVERS, PRINTERS AND STATIONERS.

www.ingramcontent.com/pod-product-compliance
Lightning Source LLC
Chambersburg PA
CBHW032226230426
43666CB00033B/1613